MW01657056

PAY ATTENTION

ARE YOU TAKING CARE OF YOUR MENTAL SELF?

JACOBY V. ARMSTRONG

ISBN-13: 978-1-954609-01-3

For information regarding special discounts for bulk purchases, please contact:

LaBoo Publishing Enterprise at staff@laboopublishing.com
www.laboopublishing.com

Dedication

Dad, thank you for your Grit and Resiliency.

Mom, thank you for your Gratitude and Ambition.

Sister, thank you for your Devotion.

Brothers, thank you for your Self-control, Confidence and Integrity.

Auntie, thank you for Clarity.

Close friends, thank you for your Compassion, Optimism, Determination, Spirituality and Sincerity.

I want to say thank you to my family, close friends and therapist. Having a circle of family and friends that you can count on day in and day out is essential in life. Thank you for your understanding and support.

Mom & Dad, I just wanted to say thank you for everything you do. This book is dedicated to the both of you.
I love you.

Rest in Peace to my Angels.

Save the Turtles.

Table of Contents

Introduction

Mental Health needs more sunlight, more candor, and more unashamed conversation.

The purpose of this handbook is to educate the reader about mental health, while sharing my personal experiences. Many times, mental illness goes undiagnosed, unresolved, and then leads to many different behaviors, which include death by suicide.

This disease is real. There are no age limits, specificity with gender or race. I want you, the reader, to feel as if you can open up and talk about your emotions, feelings, and get help. Getting help does not mean you are weak or crazy, it means YOUR Mental Health Matters. PAY ATTENTION!

“JaCoby drives the lane and BOOM!! JaCoby Armstrong just took off in the lane, for the monstrous dunk!” The announcer yells! The crowd is going crazy as I just threw down the BIG TIME SLAM! As I am jogging back to play defense, the crowd is celebrating the Dunk. As I let out a big sigh of relief, all I say to myself is, “breathe, JaCoby breathe and let’s go have fun!”

PAY ATTENTION!

Two hours prior, I was in the locker room getting ready for the basketball game. My mind is racing, my feet will not stop moving and my nerves are extremely high. Many thoughts are running around in my head and I cannot seem to calm down nor relax. I try to listen to music, but it is not calming my thoughts down fast enough! I ask myself, “Coby, what are you worried about?” As I’m thinking of millions of different answers that are running through my mind, I repeat the phrase, “Just relax and go play”. However, sometimes it is just not that simple.

Chapter One

What is Mental Health?

I will begin by defining what mental health IS NOT. Mental Health is not a sign of craziness or weakness. Mental health is the state of your emotional, psychological, physical and social well-being. This is important to understand because throughout your life, mental health will affect your thought process, mood, behavior, and overall, how you will live your life daily. Family history, life experiences, and biological factors are all elements that contribute to your state of mental health.

Understanding your emotional, psychological, physical and social well-being is very important. However, I will add one additional element, your spiritual (not religious) well-being is vital. I hope I did not lose anyone! Let me take a deeper dive into this.

What is well-being? The Centers for Disease Control and Prevention (CDC) states well-being integrates mental health (mind) and physical health (body).[1] I define well-being as your overall make-up. Medically the term DNA is used, for me I reference WB – well-being.

Have you taken the time to understand your well-being? Have you taken time to understand your mental self? Pay Attention!

---

1 Centers for Disease Control and Prevention (CDC); https://www.cdc.gov/hrqol/wellbeing.htm

Chapter Two
Types of Mental Illness

There are seven different types of classified mental disorders. The classifications are mood disorders (such as bipolar disorder or depression), substance abuse disorders, trauma related disorder (such as post-traumatic stress disorder), anxiety disorder, psychotic disorder (such as schizophrenia), personality disorder and eating disorder.

Below are examples of some disorders. There are others but these are closely associated to family and/or close friends.

Anxiety Disorder

Anxiety is what we feel when we are worried about something or someone, tensed or afraid, particularly about things that are about to happen, or which we think could happen in the future. Anxiety itself is a normal human feeling. Did you know this? The disorder arises when the intensity elevates and anxiety "attacks" surface. This typically occurs when psychological or physical conditions are triggered or develop. It is possible to experience high levels of anxiety without having a specific and/or proper diagnosis.

Generalized Anxiety Disorder (GAD) is characterized by persistent and excessive worry about a number of different things.[2] People with GAD may anticipate disaster and may be overly concerned about money, health, family, work, or other issues. Individuals with GAD find it difficult to control their worry. This type of disorder causes one to expect the worst when there is no apparent reason for concern. Additional

2 Anxiety and Depression Association of America (ADAA) https://adaa.org/understanding-anxiety/generalized-anxiety-disorder-gad

characteristics of this disorder include over-preparing for something, avoiding preparing and planning. GAD is treatable. There are licensed centers, therapists and clinicians who offer supportive and interpersonal therapies to help cope with this type of disorder.

Obsessive-compulsive disorder is another type of anxiety disorder. The term is misused in today's society. For example, you might hear someone reference another as having" OCD"' if they like things to be extremely neat and tidy. The reality is this type of disorder is far more complex and serious than many assume.

OCD has characteristics of unreasonable thoughts and fears which many times can be uncontrollable and can lead to compulsive behaviors. Behaviors focused on germs are typically associated with this disorder. The need to clean and arrange/organize objects in a compelling manner are typical signs of this disorder. 5.4% of today's population were found to have some form of an obsessive-compulsive disorder. Treatments include but are not limited to medications and/or talk therapy.

Psychotic Disorder

Psychotic Disorders are associated with disconnection from reality. The most common type of psychotic disorder is schizophrenia although there are other forms. This type of disorder many times can go undiagnosed, as symptoms are similar to other medical diagnosis. Symptoms associated with this diagnosis include but are not limited to Psychosis (such as hallucinations or delusions)

- disorganized thinking and speech
- feeling disconnected from your feelings
- difficulty concentrating
- wanting to avoid people
- a lack of interest in things

Psychiatric professionals have varying views on schizophrenia, its definition and use of the name. An estimated 4.9% of people will commit suicide, a rate that is far greater than the general population, with the highest risk of suicide occurring in the early stages of illness.

[3]Early warning signs of a psychosis disorder include:

- Worrisome drop in grades or job performance
- New trouble thinking clearly or concentrating
- Suspicious, paranoid ideas, or uneasiness with others
- Withdrawing socially, spending a lot more time alone than usual
- Unusual, overly intense new ideas, strange feelings or having no feelings at all
- Decline in self-care or personal hygiene
- Difficulty telling reality from fantasy
- Confused speech or trouble communicating

Personality disorders

Personality disorder is a type of mental health problem where your attitudes, beliefs and behaviors cause you longstanding problems in your life. Personality disorders are among the most difficult forms of mental illness to treat. Often, people with these disorders do

---

3 National Institute of Mental Health, https://www.nimh.nih.gov/health/topics/schizophrenia

not seek help because they are able to function in their day-to-day lives.

If you have this diagnosis it does not mean that you are fundamentally different from other people – but you may regularly have trouble with how you think about yourself and others and find it very difficult to change these unwanted patterns. The most common personality disorders are borderline personality disorder, paranoid personality disorder, antisocial personality disorder, obsessive- compulsive disorder, schizoid personality disorder and narcissistic personality disorder. [4]The US National Institute of Health (NIH) cites the following:

- Borderline Personality Disorder (BPD): 1.6% of US adult population suffers from this disorder.
- Antisocial personality disorder affects 1% of US adult population.
- Avoidant personality disorder affects 5.2% of US adult population.
- Personality disorder affects 9.1% of US adult population.

4 The US National Institute of Health (NIH)

Most people feel sad or irritable from time to time. Many of us have our good days and our bad days. Sometimes we just do not want to get out of bed. Can you relate? Have you ever had continuous days/weeks feeling just down and out?

A mood disorder affects a person's everyday emotional state. Shifts in emotional, mood and activity levels are symptoms associated with a mood disorder. Nearly one in ten adults (18 and older) are diagnosed with some type of mood disorder. This includes depression and bipolar disorders. Mood disorder causes unusual movements in energy, mood and activity levels. Movements range from periods of extremely "up" irritable or energized behaviors (manic episodes) to periods of extremely "low" or down behaviors (depressive episodes) such as feeling sad, hopeless or not fitting in.

Bipolar disorder (formerly referred to as manic-depressive illness) is a type of mood disorder that alters one's mood. On occasion diagnoses are made during childhood; however, they are usually made in teen or adult years. There are different levels (types) of bipolar disorder:

- Bipolar one (1) disorder. This level includes emotional and/or manic-depressive episodes that last a minimum of 7 days or mood episodes that lead up to hospitalization. Episodes of depression with mixed features (having depressive symptoms and manic symptoms at the same time) are also possible.

- Bipolar two (2) disorder. If diagnosis is made at this level, there would have been/are patterns of depressive and hypomanic episodes.

- Cyclothymic disorder (also called cyclothymia). [5]Defined by periods of hypomanic symptoms as well as periods of depressive symptoms lasting for at least 2 years (1 year in children and adolescents). However, the symptoms do not meet the diagnostic requirements for a hypomanic episode and a depressive episode.

5 National Institute of Mental Health. https://www.nimh.nih.gov/health

Chapter Three
My Story

My Dad always told me "Don't let anybody see you weak." Nobody sees that I'm weak, but deep down inside I am going through a lot. Hell is turning over.
– Kelly Oubre, Jr.

My Mom and Dad share stories of how I was born at five months and had to stay in the NICU for almost three months. I was so small I could fit in the palm of my dad's hand. I could never imagine being so small that a normal infant bottle nipple could not fit in my mouth, considering as I entered school, I was always the tallest kid in the class! Over my life, I outgrew my dad, brother, many uncles and other kids in my class. Not that I did not embrace being tall, but sometimes being the "tallest" kid in the class began to have a stronghold on me.

Being tall wasn't the only thing I was known for. I had a HUGE stuttering problem. I struggled in every element involving speaking. I remember in elementary school when the teacher called on me and I had to read something, I used to die inside because I knew I was going to stutter which always lead to the whole class laughing at me. I was so embarrassed that I asked the teacher not to call on me to read because I did not want the other students laughing at me.

Over time, I learned to embrace my height and to use it to excel in sports as a student-athlete. However, because I stuttered so much, I began to shut down and talk less in fear of being made fun of. Even now, at the age of 25, I find myself struggling from time to time. Over the years, I have turned what I considered one of my biggest flaws into something that I empower and embrace.

One of my first triggers in my mental health journey, although I did not know it at the time, was the death of my great grandmother. I think it affected me because of how my mom was affected. It was my first experience of death of a family member that I can recall that affected me in some traumatic way.

My second trigger, again there was not a diagnosis made at the time, is when I was about to enter college. I experienced a death that shook my soul! My aunt Tarsha passed away, to me unexpectedly. The evening of my college tour, my dad received the phone call that his sister passed. My Aunt Tarsha died – are you serious? We ultimately ended the school tour and made arrangements to return home immediately. There were no words. Pay Attention!

The same year one of best friend's mom passed. Yes, this was another trigger as she was another close supporter of mine. To see my best friend lose his mom, I could not grasp hold of this. I sat back and wanted to make sure I was there for him. To see my best friend go through so much pain, it was hard to fight back the tears because of how close my friend and I were and still are to this day. To know he was hurting made me hurt too.

The next year my great grandfather passed. Not again!! Another death. Seeing my family display their reactions and pain really got to me. I just wanted all my family to be okay, but I had to understand that death is hard.

The same year I found out my great Uncle had cancer. Now do not get me wrong, but I was so tired of hearing about deaths related to cancer. My last visit with my uncle was profound to me. Here I was in college, texting him every day and always checking up on him the best way I could. Next thing you know, I received a call saying "JaCoby, Uncle Earl has passed". At that point, I was really in a dark place mentally. I became severely depressed and began having dark thoughts. I was trying to help myself while also trying to be there for my family the best way I knew how. Pay Attention!

The following year my daddy called me to tell me one of "my biggest supporters" died – Mr. Oscar. My dad was heartbroken and so was I. My dad always spoke about how Mr. "O" use to watch ALL my games. I knew my dad was hurting and I wanted to be there for him.

That same year, my second cousin, who was really like my first cousin, as we were close in age, died in an auto accident. At this point, I was experiencing severe depression and now I had to deal with another death. Now, understand, she and I did not talk everyday however I was very close with her sister. Death is not easy for anyone, and people handle it differently. My concern was being there for her. She lost her sister. Can you imagine that? Pay Attention!

As time passed, I became numb. I began to isolate myself and started to not care about life and many people in my life, if I am being honest. I just did not care. I entered counseling, which with prayer saved my life. I learned about life triggers and how to deal with not only grief, but I began learning a lot about myself and then more news…

"JaCoby, Poo died." My Uncle Rodrick, nicknamed Poo, was the light on my dad's side of the family. This was unexpected and occurred the day my parents were hosting my cousin's graduation party. My paternal grandmother was in the hospital dealing with cancer and her baby boy had died! For me, this was the hardest death I had to deal with thus far. Not only was his death an unexpected tragic accident, but the death affected the whole family in many ways. I felt hopeless, lost, and just wanted to be present for my family. All I could think about was being there for my dad. I needed to be there for him. I worried about my mom, however her strength and honor to my grandmother surpassed all. This loss shook us all including my grandmother, our Gigi.

My grandmother was staying with us as she had cancer and had reached a point where she needed assistance in some areas. It was funny at times as my grandmother always lifted you up by throwing a PRAYER on you, even if you didn't know it. In her last days, my entire family, especially my mom and dad, were fully vested in making sure she and our family were all-good.

When grandma died, I worried about my mom, dad, brother and sister more than myself. But I was hurt. She told me I would go overseas and be great and have much success. I was her CobyCo! Her FAITH helped me through many rough times. She taught me about the value of being peaceful within. Having that internal peace is vital. But now she was gone. Pay Attention!

Through all the deaths year after year, it was hard for mc. Somc days were easy and then some days were difficult. There have been many times that I have found myself drowning in my mind. Every time I started the process to grieve for one death, another happened. Most of the time I was away from home at school or playing overseas. The distance factor is always hard. Many times, I regretted being away because I tend to expect the worst and always wanted to be there for my family during hard times. When you hear the anguish and see the tears and pain of the people you love over and over again it tends to do something to you.

During my journey, I began to learn more about the importance of mental health. I was able to learn more about my diagnosis, post-traumatic stress disorder and ADHD.

How do I cope? Stress disorder? Believe me, I found myself feeling some type of way, however I was somewhat relieved. Sharing the news with mom and dad and other family members, took more weight from me. As I began therapy, one thing I wanted to learn was how to be present for my family without losing myself. I have not fully mastered this, but I learned the importance of self-care. Ensuring my mental self is safe and sound is my number one priority. We have to remember and understand that life gets overwhelming at times. Sometimes as human beings we do not know how to deal with it and that's okay. When I was going through my darkest times mentally and emotionally, I felt like I was in a pitch-black room and couldn't get out. There was a glimpse of light, but it always faded away. I felt like I was trapped in my own mind. Seeing a therapist was one of the best decisions I made for myself. Mental illness is no joke. Mental Health is very important. Your Mental Self Matters. Pay Attention!

Chapter Four
Living with Mental Illness

Living with a mental illness is different every day. Some days can be bad, and some days are good. For me, I have learned to embrace my overall mental self. I struggle with anxiety day to day. Some days my anxiety levels are high and some days they are very low. However, my anxiety is always present. To help me cope with this, I enjoy playing basketball, watching animal planet and listening to music. Over the past couple years, I have made tremendous growth in dealing with my anxieties. I continue to learn ways for me not to worry about things I cannot control. The key to regulating any form of anxiety is to not worry or stress about anything you cannot control and trust that it will work itself out. Pay Attention!

Over time, I have continued to learn about my trauma of the repeated deaths I experienced of close family members and friends. These traumas triggered a level of post-traumatic stress disorder commonly referred to as PTSD. PTSD is a form of stress and anxiety disorder. These types of disorders are triggered by experiencing sudden or unexpected events such as the deaths I experienced. Symptoms include having flashbacks of reliving the trauma repeatedly and racing heart palpitations. Living with PTSD can be very tricky at times. At first, it was extremely hard. There are times when I get triggered and my whole mood goes down causing the whole day to be ruined. Sometimes the stress disorder would linger and affect me the next couple days. There are times when you want to be alone, listen to music and just cry. I would get so down on myself. I would be reminiscing about the good and bad memories shared. Along with PTSD, over the years I have been diagnosed with chronic insomnia and ADHD. Insomnia is the inability to fall and stay asleep. Being an athlete and having insomnia is a bad combination to have. It's hard enought to walk into practice and give it your all if you have slept well all night. It's a mental battle everyday to be at my best and then to get enough sleep each night. It's no joke.

No matter how big or small the obstacle is, you have to push through it! Pay Attention!

Upon learning about my diagnosis, I automatically began to conduct additional research to understand more about this. I learned the best way to limit episodes of PTSD, is to start by identifying my triggers. Once I identified my triggers, I began to learn how to deal with them. An example is when I hear a song that reminds me of someone who has passed, I stop whatever I am doing, take a deep breath, I might cry, but I just sit calmly and begin to think of positive reinforcements to the trigger(s). Whether it is a smile, a quote, something to ensure it is a positive reinforcement. The same method I used to help me with PTSD, I use when my anxiety levels are high. Through counseling, I have learned that the key is to identify the triggers and then learn how to deal with them when they present themselves.

Over time, I have found myself thinking about my family members and I begin to smile, reminiscing on some positive aspect of my relationship with them. Breathing is important and learning to take time for myself. I still worry about my family, but my FAITH overwhelmingly exceeds the PAIN.

In terms of my insomnia, I learned through counseling and a sleep study that my brain was hyperactive at night. This really means that my anxiety levels were rising and did not allow me to sleep. I would lay in the bed for hours trying to get to sleep and next thing I knew, I would be watching the sun come up. In dealing with my insomnia, I had to learn how to lower my anxiety level at night. Ultimately, I found that writing in a journal before bed helped tremendously. What do I write in the journal? Anything and everything that is on my mind at that exact moment. It's like casting my worries and thoughts onto a piece of paper. When I do this, I feel the anxiety exit my body. It's like a huge sigh of relief and I can finally breathe.

Living with mental illness now, I love it. I embrace it. Sounds strange huh? Understanding ME and knowing about ME is soothing to my soul. Sure, some days are harder than others, but the self-reflection is the best part. For me, looking back knowing that I overcame depression, stuttering, and I am learning how to live a healthy lifestyle mentally while having PTSD and ADHD is truly a blessing.

Chapter Five

Don't Be Afraid...

Can you relate to any area I have discussed? Do you feel like you cannot talk to anybody about your feelings? Do you feel sad or mad? Do you have really bad anxiety? Maybe you also have dealt with one or many deaths that have you feeling somewhat defeated. If you think you might be dealing with some form of mental illness, do not be afraid, let's take the next step, I am here with you. Do not be afraid to let your parents, coach or counselor know, you might need to seek therapy. You are not alone! You are not crazy (I do not like to use this word) nor are you by yourself.

I want you to really think about your well-being. Ask yourself are you being your best self? Are you happy? Do not feel ashamed to speak up and out and ask for help. In all my classes, I was never encouraged to examine myself for mental health. I get it, I was the person who said I would never go to a counselor to receive help. I held my emotions and feelings inside for plenty of years and that is very unhealthy. Even if it's just to vent and talk to somebody sometimes it feels good to get that weight off your shoulders.

Are you having thoughts of harming yourself or others? Are you experiencing thoughts of killing yourself? I know many people do not like to talk about suicide, but it is real. I was there. Some people you see every day could be there also.

Let me ask you this, do you have a strong enough relationship with your parent(s) to discuss your mental health with them? If not, what about a teacher or your coach? Just take the next step and talk to someone. Remember, you can't reach your full potential in life when you have a negative mental capacity.

This does not only apply to individuals who might be or are struggling mentally. It applies to everybody. And if you are someone who has overcome and consider yourself to be mentally sound – HELP SOMEONE who is not. Check on your parents. Check on your friends. Check on everybody you love and care about! Sometimes a simple text message or phone call can change a person's whole mood. Implement self-care into your lifestyle to create a healthier mind, body and spirit.

Chapter Six

In Conclusion

In conclusion, I want to say my goal in writing this handbook was not to overwhelm you with a lot of words but to show references to mental illness that you can associate with. This is my story. Millions of other people also have their own stories. Although I reference students and student-athletes, my prayer is, if anyone reads this and feels they need help, that they will take the next step and get help. If that is only one person – then I can say I have continued to help somebody.

I did not detail all forms of mental illnesses and behaviors but wanted to open the conversation and dialogue. It is real!

Accepting that you have a mental illness does not mean you don't have FAITH in a higher power; it does not mean you are less than anyone else. It simply means you are dealing with some form of emotion or behavior that you need help controlling. Your FAITH sustains you through your mental health journey. Pay Attention!

If you have made it this far I commend you. You are interested in helping YOU! Learn to control and overcome your mental health and implement self-care into your lifestyle. Keep taking steps to educate yourself and others around you on taking your mental health seriously. Talk to someone who can help you. Sometimes it is good to reflect on how far you have come mentally.

If you are reading this right now and you have not told anybody about your mental health battles, then now is the time. Do not try to hold all your feelings inside. If you do not take the next steps, I assure you one day you will explode in some form or fashion. You must learn techniques to be able to release stress. You have to value self-care.

You have to let it out and talk to somebody. Reach out to your mom, dad, teacher, coach, doctor or anybody in your life that will not only listen but also help you. If you do not have anyone to talk to please email me. I will listen. Things happen in your life that are not your fault; things that you cannot control.

Please email me at selfcarepayattention1@gmail.com. I will listen and I will make sure you get some help. Things happen in our lives that are not our fault. Sometimes somebody just needs someone to listen. Not everyone has mental health issues, but many times people deal with things that can be overwhelming and it is perfectly fine to seek help. Please take care of your mental health.

Believe in yourself. Love yourself. Nobody is perfect.

Nothing in this world can stop you from being successful except you. Do not let mental health hold you back. Your mind controls your body. If you have an unbalanced and negative mind, the body will always follow. Everybody around you has a story. Everybody has their own trials and tribulations. You have to educate yourself and learn the proper way to seek help when you have experienced anything that can set you back mentally. Once you learn to overcome your mental health battles, you can help others that are in the same or similar situation.

At the end of the day, everyone has their own problems, issues, and flaws. These do not define YOU. Remember to always Pay Attention!

About The Author

JaCoby Armstrong is a Professional Basketball player currently playing overseas. He is a powerful force on and off the court and uses his positive attitude and tireless energy to encourage others to work hard and succeed.

Born to Marla and Clemente Armstrong on February 12, 1995 at 21 weeks in Dallas, Texas, JaCoby learned early on how to push through and overcome. Even after the doctors and nurses in the NICU counted him out, he surpassed all medical understanding. He spent his high school and college years participating in mentorship to youth of all ages. While in college, he began his own mentorship in addition to the community service required by athletics. To date he remains in contact with many of his mentees.

JaCoby excelled in football and basketball. During the start of his 9th grade year at Wylie High School in Wylie, Texas, the decision was made for him to focus solely on basketball. Armstrong was a key component of the school's basketball team earning year over year basketball recognition, having the honor of playing alongside his older brother, Jordan. During the 2010-2011 school year, he was 1st Team All District in addition to being the leader of the state of 4A in Rebounds with 11.3 rebounds per game.

Armstrong's basketball prowess earned him a full athletic scholarship to The University of New Hampshire in 2013. During his time there he was instrumental in helping the team become the all-time winningest basketball team in UNH basketball history. After completing his undergraduate degree and post graduate studies, JaCoby made the decision to further his basketball career by playing professionally overseas.

JaCoby signed with the Mgzavrebi-Armia Tbilisi in the Georgia – Superleague. He had a season high of 24 points in 35 minutes. He scored double figure 15 times in 18 games while scoring 20 points or more in four games. Armstrong then signed to play for Romania's Liga Nationala. He scored an average of 14.7 points and 5.1 rebounds within 24 minutes.

Outside of his career in basketball, JaCoby has just accomplished one of his goals – becoming a published author. In addition, he has partnered with his siblings to form J-Flyy, Inc. an innovative apparel company focused on increasing empowerment through fashion and charity. Empowering others is very important to JaCoby. He continues to mentor others while building a forum to allow them the opportunity to speak about life issues, including mental illness.

Made in the USA
Monee, IL
07 March 2021

61154561R00026